DREAMS CAN HELP

A Journal Guide to Understanding Your Dreams and Making Them Work for You

Jonni Kincher

Edited by Mary Morse

Free Spirit PUBLISHING

Library of Congress Cataloging-in-Publication Data
Kincher, Jonni, 1949–
    Dreams can help: a journal guide to understanding your dreams and making them work for you / Jonni Kincher: edited by Mary Morse
    p. cm.
    Bibliography: p.
    Includes index.
    ISBN 0-915793-15-6
    1. Dreams. I. Morse, Mary. II. Title.
BF1091.K46   1988
154.6'3--dc19   88-7630
                                    CIP

10 9 8 7 6 5 4 3
Printed in the United States of America

Cover and book design by MacLean and Tuminelly
Cover and text illustrations by Roy Staeck
Border illustrations by MacLean and Tuminelly
Supervising editor: Pamela Espeland

Free Spirit Publishing Inc.
400 First Avenue North, Suite 616
Minneapolis, MN 55401
(612) 338-2068 / (800) 735-7323

Dedication

My Grandma Vesta always told me that she considered a day wasted if she didn't learn something new. This book is dedicated to that spirit and dream which kept her young for all of her 97 years, to all of the kids who helped my own dreams come true for Psychology for Kids, and to the young at heart, whose curiosity keeps the world alive with new ideas and possible dreams.

Contents

Acknowledgments

I am grateful to the F.L.A.S.H. Program initiated by Kristen Thibedeau in Redlands, California. There I got started on my path. Thanks to Oregon's Saturday Academy, especially to Catherine Lauer, I have been able to continue and expand my work.

To students, whose questioning sharpened my insight and inspired me, I owe a debt of thanks. To their parents who supported them and me, I am also very grateful.

To all at Free Spirit Publishing, especially Judy Galbraith, thanks for helping make a dream a reality through expert communication, hard work, and an uncanny sense of timing.

To my own family for supporting my work and trying my many projects, thanks, for I could not have done it without you!

Introduction

What was the *best* dream you ever had? Were you flying through the air like a bird? Winning first prize at a piano recital? Driving a race car? Opening presents under a Christmas tree?

What was the *worst* dream you ever had? Were you being chased by monsters? Falling down a deep, dark hole? Trying to call for help but unable to make a sound?

What was the *silliest* dream you ever had? Were you walking to school in your pajamas? Making your parents do homework? Having a conversation with your cat?

We all dream. Every one of us, every night, whether we realize it or not. You may not remember your dreams, but they happen anyway. Good dreams, bad dreams, funny dreams, sad dreams. Dreams that repeat the past and dreams that seem to predict the future. Dreams that puzzle you and dreams that give you answers.

Do your dreams matter? Are the things you dream about related to your waking life? People who study human behavior think so. They believe that your dreams can help you discover why you feel and act the way you do.

You don't have to tell someone else your dreams to find out what they mean. That's because *you* are the best interpreter of your dreams. Most dreams are linked to very recent events and emotions in your life. Who knows the most about what has happened to you? Who knows the most about your feelings? Not your parents, not your teachers, not your friends — but you!

Understanding your dreams can help you understand *yourself*. Your dreams can help you solve problems, get along better with your family and friends, and reach your personal goals. But before you can understand your dreams, you have to remember them, and the best way to remember them is to write them down as soon as possible after you dream them.

This book shows you how to start and keep your own Dream Journal. Along the way, it introduces you to lots of fascinating facts about dreams and dreaming, a few famous dreamers, and kids like you who have learned how to interpret their dreams.

If you've always been interested in dreams...if you want to know more about why you dream and what your dreams can mean...if you want to find out more about yourself...then *Dreams Can Help* is for you.

Good luck, have fun, and may your best dreams come true.

Jonni Kincher

A Special Note to Parents and Teachers

I have worked both as a parent and a teacher with children and their dreams. As a parent, I have found closer communication with my own children through dream discussions. We could talk more openly at times about the misadventures and feelings of "dream characters" than we could about our own waking feelings. In talking about our dreams, we were really sharing an intimate side of our emotional lives.

As a teacher, I have found that dream discussions with groups of children can be based on the same analytical thinking approach used for analyzing literature. This has allowed many non-readers to expand their horizons.

Dreams are a rich educational resource available to everyone. Children are naturally curious and often frightened by their dreams. When encouraged to share them, they *will* share them — at first, perhaps, to relieve their fears, and later because sharing them has proven to be fun and interesting.

In my own experience, different age groups require different approaches.

• Ages 2-7

I would not recommend working with children of this age in dream groups. However, the smaller family setting is appropriate. Children who are gifted, mature for their age, or highly verbal may benefit from a group experience by age 6 or 7.

When working with very young children, encourage them to create from their dreams. Enter into the fantasy with them and experience it. A child might act out a dream or take the role of a "director." He or she could make abstract representations of the dream with fingerpaints or clay. This should be fun for the child while stimulating the development of verbal skills and abstract thinking processes.

• Ages 8-12

The groups of children I have worked with have been within this age range. Many of the sections and exercises in this book have been specifically designed for them, but you may adapt them for different ages.

Children between 8 and 12 readily work with dreams. They are more verbal than their younger counterparts and less guarded than their older counterparts.

- **Ages 13 and over**

These children will be able to deal with dream material in a more sophisticated manner since they are at a higher verbal level and have had more life experiences. This advantage is offset by their natural guardedness against the adult world. This is all the more reason to use dreams as a bridge to communication. Approach the materials in a game-like manner rather than seriously. Keep in mind that children in this age group are sometimes best related to as adults, and at other times best related to as children. The sensitive adult will know how to judge this variable.

As you work with the children in your home or classroom, keep these four guidelines in mind:

1. NEVER force a child to reveal his or her dreams to you or to a group. Dreams are personal and should only be shared when the dreamer feels comfortable.

2. NEVER read a child's Dream Journal without his or her *express* permission. Just as it is unethical to read someone else's diary without first clearing it with him or her, a Dream Journal is private, and that privacy should be respected. Be sure to communicate this to the child.

3. NEVER interpret dreams according to some set "formula" — for example, "Horses mean danger." This can be frightening to the dreamer, and it is also absurd because each object in a dream has a whole set of meanings unique to the dreamer and the dreamer's set of life circumstances. The dreamer is the interpreter, and no one else.

4. ALWAYS listen to a dreamer with an open and generous mind. Remember that he or she is sharing very personal thoughts and experiences freely and willingly. When you hear a dream, you're receiving a gift of trust.

I hope the methods and experiences described in this book will be of value to you and the young ones in your care.

Part 1

DREAMS AND DREAMING

"Into the land of
dreams I long to go."
Mary Coleridge

Getting Started

Do you remember many of your dreams, or only a few? *Dreams Can Help* will show you how to remember more of your dreams than ever before. But first...

Write your best dream here

What happened? Where did it take place? What did you do? Who else was in it besides you? Describe the "landscape" of your dream — the things and colors and people you saw. Then tell why this was your best dream ever...so far.

Dream Times

When do you dream?

That may seem like a silly question. Naturally you dream when you're asleep! But dream researchers have learned that you dream at *very specific times* when you're asleep.

Your sleep is divided into NREM times (for "**N**on-**R**apid-**E**y**e**-**M**ove-ment") and REM times (for "**R**apid-**E**y**e**-**M**ovement"). During REM times, your eyes move back and forth under your eyelids. You may smile, frown, or jerk your legs or arms. You may whimper or mutter words.

Most of the dreaming you do takes place when you're in REM sleep.

Nobody knew much about REM sleep until 1952. In that year, three University of Chicago researchers were studying the sleep patterns of babies. Each baby had electrodes taped to its scalp that were connected to a writing instrument called a *polygraph*. The polygraph recorded brain wave signals with wavy lines on a roll of graph paper.

(This technique of recording brain activity — called an EEG, for "electroencephalogram" — is still used today for sleep research. EEGs are also important tools in the diagnosis and treatment of epilepsy and other brain disorders.)

Nathaniel Kleitman, Eugene Aserinsky, and William Dement, the three researchers, noticed something unusual about the sleeping babies. The normal brain wave pattern of gentle swells was frequently interrupted with sharp bursts of "awake" activity. They started watching the babies closely when these bursts of brain activity occurred. The babies' eyes and bodies moved! Later the three men discovered more physical evidence that connected these bursts of brain activity to the arousal of the nervous system.

Stage 0 (awake)

Stage 4 (deep sleep)

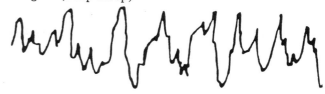

Stage REM

True or False?

"The older you get, the more you dream."

Answer:

This statement is FALSE. Everyone dreams, but babies dream the *most* and older people dream the *least*.

Newborn babies spend nearly nine hours each day in REM or dreaming sleep. Researchers think that babies dream so much because they have to learn a lot quickly. Of course, since babies cannot tell us about their dreams, this connection between dreams and learning is still just a theory.

How much time do *you* spend dreaming each day? (NOT including the time you spend daydreaming!) Find out from this chart:*

If you are	You spend this much time dreaming
0-24 months old	9 hours a day
2-5 years old	2 1/2 hours a day
5-50 years old	1 1/2 hours a day
50 years and older	1 hour a day

* This information is from Patricia Garfield, *Your Child's Dreams* (New York: Ballantine Books, 1984), page 11.

Kleitman, Aserinsky, and Dement started studying adults to find out if the same nervous system arousal happened in them. Because adults could talk about their experiences, the three men were able to prove what they suspected: REM sleep was dreaming sleep! When adults were awakened during REM times, they always talked about their dreams.

What these University of Chicago researchers learned completely changed scientific thinking about sleeping and dreaming.

Brain Waves

Brain waves are the electrical energy generated by your brain. Different types of brain waves reflect different physical states and emotions. Some brain waves are slow and some are fast. Each type has a name.

- **Alpha waves** are the ones that occur as you first close your eyes and relax.

- **Beta waves** indicate "awake" activity.

- **Theta waves** are slow waves that indicate the beginning of sleep.

- **Delta waves** are very slow waves that indicate deep sleep.

Think of your brain as a country divided into the "states" of Alpha, Beta, Theta, and Delta. Then imagine the feelings evoked by each of these brain waves as "towns" in your "states" of mind.

Try describing your moods in brain wave "code." For example, when you're feeling "grouchy," say you're feeling "beta." Instead of being "puzzled," you're "theta." And when you're really feeling lazy and relaxed, you're "alpha."

What is brain wave "code" for these feelings?

- angry
- powerful
- curious
- upset
- drowsy

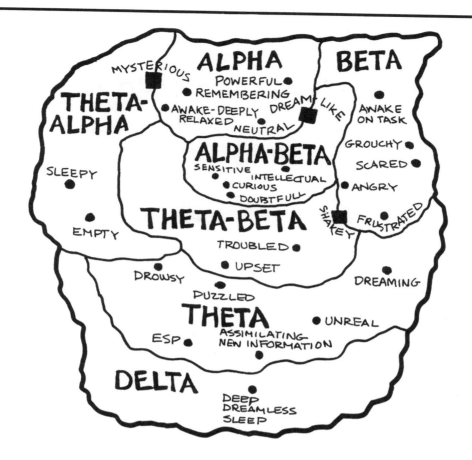

The Colors of Your Dreams

Many people claim that they only dream in black-and-white. But researchers have found that we really dream in color — mostly in green and red.

Do you remember the colors of your dreams? If you don't, you're not alone. Unless a specific color is an important element in the content of a dream, you probably won't remember it upon waking.

Scientists have learned that colors can affect our emotions. Some colors make us feel calm, while others make us feel anxious. Certain colors are believed to symbolize certain feelings. For example:

- **Green** = life — or jealousy, as in "green-eyed monster."

- **Red** = excitement. (Maybe that's why so many fast-food restaurants are decorated in red and orange.)

- **Black** = evil or death.

- **White** = innocence, purity, or newness.

Many dream researchers don't think that the colors people see in their dreams are all that important — unless they see the same colors over and over again.

Can you remember the colors of your dreams? What do you think those colors mean? Have you ever dreamed about red mountains, blue people — or purple cows?

Write your most colorful dream here

What happened? Where did it take place? What were some of the
colors you saw? How did those colors make you feel?

Do You Dream What You Eat?

Nutritionists say *yes*. Think about the last time you spent an evening at a fair or an amusement park. You probably stuffed yourself on cotton candy and hot dogs and soda, went on dizzying rides, came home, climbed into bed — and had nightmares. No wonder!

If what you eat affects what you dream, then maybe eating certain foods before bedtime and avoiding others is one way to control your dreams.

For example, instead of eating candy or pizza for a bedtime snack, try having a glass of milk and a cookie. Milk relaxes you. And when you feel relaxed, you're more likely to have pleasant dreams. (Could this be the reason babies love to drink warm milk at bedtime?)

Find out for yourself if you dream what you eat. Use the Snack-And-Dream Diary on pages 10 - 11 to record what you eat for a week and the kinds of dreams you have. Experiment with different kinds of snacks — an apple one night, ice cream the next, a peanut butter sandwich the next, and so on.

Don't worry *too* much about the eating-and-dreaming connection. It appears that dreams can sometimes help you make up for eating "mistakes." Some theories say that the brain works to keep you asleep by incorporating sensations into your dreams — by taking events going on in the environment or in your body and weaving them into your dreams. So if you eat something that gives you a stomach ache, you may end up having a weird and wild dream instead of waking up to feel miserable!

Talking Turkey

Brain cells communicate with one another by releasing chemical substances called *neurotransmitters*. For example, brain cells convert the tryptophan in turkey into the neurotransmitter *serotonin*. Serotonin sends a "sleep" message to your brain — which is why you may want a nap after a turkey dinner.

So maybe a slice of turkey would make a great bedtime snack, especially on nights when you're feeling wide awake.

Snack-and-Dream Diary

DAY 1

What I ate before going to bed:

I had a ☐ good dream ☐ bad dream ☐ can't remember

(If you can remember your dream, write a short description of it)

DAY 2

What I ate before going to bed:

I had a ☐ good dream ☐ bad dream ☐ can't remember

(If you can remember your dream, write a short description of it)

DAY 3

What I ate before going to bed:

I had a ☐ good dream ☐ bad dream ☐ can't remember

(If you can remember your dream, write a short description of it)

DAY 4

What I ate before going to bed:

I had a ☐ good dream ☐ bad dream ☐ can't remember

(If you can remember your dream, write a short description of it)

DAY 5

What I ate before going to bed:

I had a ☐ good dream ☐ bad dream ☐ can't remember

(If you can remember your dream, write a short description of it)

DAY 6

What I ate before going to bed:

I had a ☐ good dream ☐ bad dream ☐ can't remember

(If you can remember your dream, write a short description of it)

DAY 7

What I ate before going to bed:

I had a ☐ good dream ☐ bad dream ☐ can't remember

(If you can remember your dream, write a short description of it)

What I learned from keeping this diary:

Why Do You Dream?

Do you dream to remember? Or dream to forget? There are several famous theories about why humans spend so much of their lives sleeping and dreaming. Here are just a few:

- Dr. Sigmund Freud, the founder of modern psychoanalysis, believed that dreams are "the royal road to the unconscious." According to Freud, you dream to remember your forgotten past and get in touch with your emotions. Dreams are "memories in disguise."

- Dr. Carl Jung, student of Freud and author of *Man And His Symbols* and other books about dreaming, believed that dreams are full of universal symbols from a "collective unconscious" — a "group mind" shared by all humans. According to Jung, dreams show you these symbols to help you prepare for the next stages in your life. They are like road signs that you see long before you actually reach them, but they point you in the general right direction.

- Dr. Alfred Adler believed that you dream to create a certain emotional state. He called dreams "emotion factories," creators of moods that move dreamers to take action. In this way, he theorized, dreams can help people to solve their problems.

- Dr. Christopher Evans, a computer scientist and psychologist, believed that the brain is like a computer. You dream to "sort out" the clutter of your mind. New information is compared with old and put in its proper place, while useless information is cleared out. Dr. Evans's theory is supported by the fact that people seem to have more dreams when they are in new or unfamiliar surroundings. (Do you dream more when you are on vacation?)

- Because elderly people spend so little time dreaming, Dr. Ian Oswald thinks that dreams are used to *repair* the brain and help it grow. The younger you are, the more you need to dream.

Do you agree with any of these theories? Or do you have your own theory about why people dream?

My Theory About Why People Dream

I think people dream because:

_____
_____
_____
_____
_____
_____
_____
_____
_____
_____
_____
_____
_____
_____

Dream Facts

★ The average person has more than 1,000 dreams each year.

★ Almost all animals (including human animals) need to sleep and dream. The more complex the animal, the more REM sleep it has.

★ Plants don't "sleep" as we know it, but they do enter dormant, or "sleep-like," stages.

★ Dreams that occur during the same night are usually variations on the same subject.

★ You have four or five separate dreams each night. Unless you are awakened during REM sleep, however, you probably will remember only the last dream you had before morning.

★ Dreams stimulate your imagination and help you to function better in your daily life. Your sleeping or unconscious thoughts affect you just as much as your waking or conscious thoughts. Some psychologists believe that your sleeping thoughts influence your behavior even *more* than your waking thoughts because your brain circuits are more open to suggestions while you're asleep.

★ A certain amount of dreaming may even be *necessary*. Researchers have found that when people are deprived of REM sleep, they start to hallucinate — to see dreams while they are awake — as if to make up for the dreams they missed.

Animal Dreams

Bottlenose dolphins can stay awake and sleep at the same time! They even sleep with one eye open. This is because they have the ability to use one side of their brains at a time. For the first hour or so of sleep, they switch off their right brain. Then they wake up their right brain and turn off their left brain. The bottlenose dolphin is completely awake only when both sides of the brain are conscious.

You probably don't have a bottlenose dolphin to watch at your house. But you can find out some very interesting things about sleep and dreaming by watching your dog, cat, or pet bird. You won't know exactly what it is dreaming about, but its actions and your own knowledge of its temperament and activities will give you enough information to draw some possible conclusions.

In one survey of pet owners, dog owners said they saw many "dream symptoms" after their dogs had experienced a particularly busy or exciting day. Here are some dream symptoms you can watch for in your pet:

- Twitching of paws, whiskers or tail

- Squeaking, growling, whining, or other strange noises

- Muttering words (for parrots or other talking birds)

- Eyes rolling or twitching under closed eyelids

- Irregular or rapid breathing

- "Surprised" awakenings — the animal suddenly jumps up and looks around in confusion

One way psychologists learn about animal (and people) behavior is by careful *observation*. They simply watch and listen and record everything they see and hear. If you want to learn more about your pet, try observing it while it is sleeping. Plan to spend about five minutes a day for at least three days in a row. (For example, maybe your dog takes a nap after supper. Or maybe your cat snoozes on the windowsill at around the same time every day.) Use the Pet Observation Chart to record what you see and hear. Then draw some conclusions of your own.

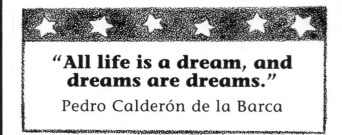

"All life is a dream, and dreams are dreams."

Pedro Calderón de la Barca

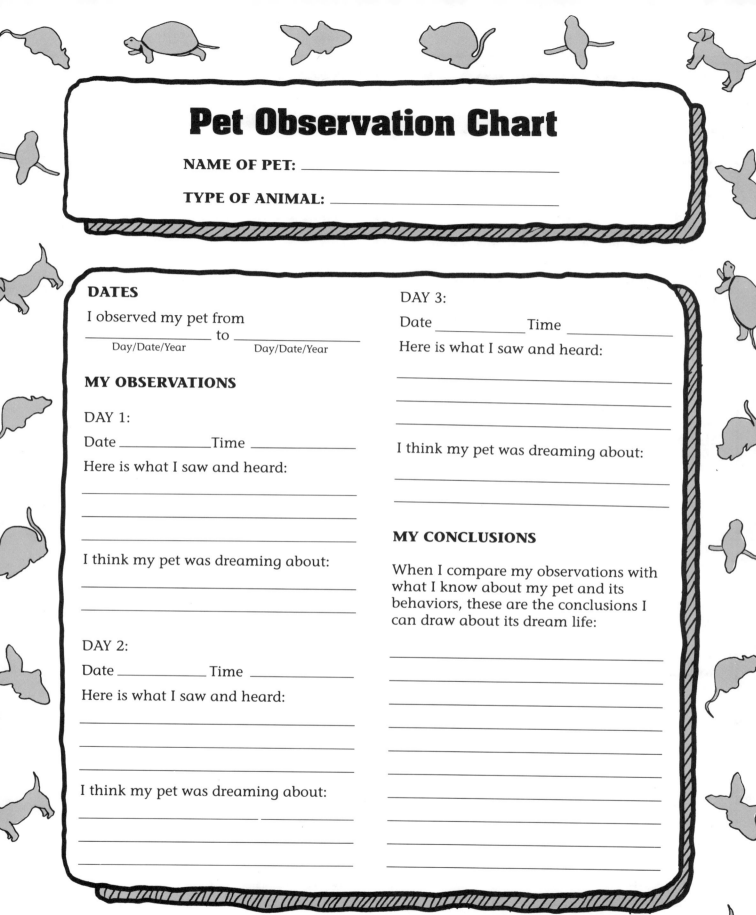

Pet Observation Chart

NAME OF PET: _____

TYPE OF ANIMAL: _____

DATES

I observed my pet from
_____ to _____
Day/Date/Year   Day/Date/Year

MY OBSERVATIONS

DAY 1:

Date _____ Time _____

Here is what I saw and heard:

_____

_____

_____

I think my pet was dreaming about:

_____

_____

DAY 2:

Date _____ Time _____

Here is what I saw and heard:

_____

_____

_____

I think my pet was dreaming about:

_____

_____

_____

DAY 3:

Date _____ Time _____

Here is what I saw and heard:

_____

_____

_____

I think my pet was dreaming about:

_____

_____

MY CONCLUSIONS

When I compare my observations with
what I know about my pet and its
behaviors, these are the conclusions I
can draw about its dream life:

_____

_____

_____

_____

_____

_____

_____

Dreams and the Senoi*

The Senoi (rhymes with "annoy") are members of a tribe that lives in the jungles of central Malaysia. When anthropologist and psychologist Kilton Stewart studied the Senoi in 1935, he learned that the tribe had not reported a violent crime for more than 200 years! People who have visited the Senoi in the years since say that they still do not need jails or police.

Why are the Senoi so peaceful? Psychologists think that it's because of their dreams, what they do about them, and the whole psychology they have built around dreams and dreaming.

The Senoi take their dreams very seriously. All members of the tribe share their dreams with one another. Instead of getting into arguments or fights, they use dream recall and interpretation to work out their differences.

The Senoi believe that you rule your own "dream world" or "spirit universe." This gives you power over yourself. Having power over yourself weakens your need to have power over other people. It also boosts your self-confidence.

To the Senoi, the dream world is a *real* world which must be dealt with

* This section on the Senoi was adapted from Kilton Stewart's chapter, "Dream Theory in Malaya," in *Altered States of Consciousness*, edited by Charles T. Tart (Garden City, NY: Doubleday, 1972), pages 161-170.

Four Senoi Dream Techniques

Here are some techniques that work for the Senoi. Try them and see if they work for you.

1. **Face your problems**. When you meet a bad dream being, don't run away from it. Instead, attack and kill it in your dream. The dream being will return as your friend.

2. **Love your enemies.** If you do something bad to someone else in a dream, tell the person about the dream the next day and apologize for what you did. Then do something nice for the person or give him or her a gift.

3. **Share your feelings**. If someone you know in real life does something bad to you in a dream, tell the person about it the next day. The Senoi believe that the person must then "make it up to you" in real life. Suggest that the person do something nice for you or give you a gift.

4. **Learn to recognize your friends**. A true friend will never harm you, even in a dream. If you dream about a friend who does something bad to you, you're not really dreaming about your friend. Instead, you're dreaming about a bad dream being wearing the mask of a friend. Understanding this can help you to avoid bad feelings about your friend.

and understood. This world is inhabited by negative feelings which the Senoi call "dream beings." (We call these negative feelings "anger," "jealousy," "fear," "hate," and so on.) The Senoi believe that each member of the tribe must help the others to defeat their dream beings. But before you can get someone to help you in your dreams, you must *first* help that person in waking life.

Every morning, Senoi fathers and older brothers listen to and analyze the dreams that the younger children remember and describe. Later in the day, the adults and older children gather to discuss their dreams. They also share their family's dreams with the rest of the tribe. This keeps everyone in the tribe in close touch with everyone else.

Maybe there's a message here for the rest of us. Maybe if we shared our dreams with one another, we could work out our problems without arguments, fights — or wars.

Dreams and the Naskapi*

Like the Senoi, the Naskapi Indians of Canada's Labrador Peninsula also take their dreams very seriously. They see the soul as an inner companion which they call the "Great Man."

* This section on the Naskapi was adapted from Carl Jung, *Man And His Symbols* (New York: Doubleday and Company, Reprint Edition 1979), pages 161, 162 and 208.

The Naskapi believe that the Great Man wants them to understand their dreams and test the "truths" they discover in their dreams. In return, the Great Man sends them more and better dreams.

The Naskapi "fix" their dreams in real life by turning the dreams they remember into works of art or other creations. In this way they give their dreams a concrete presence and value.

Here are some suggestions for Dream Creations. (Or dream up your own!)

- Come up with a Dream Invention.
- Write a Dream Play.
- Make a Dream Sculpture out of clay.
- Do a Dream Painting.
- Bake Dream Cookies (or a Dream Cake).
- Compose a Dream Song, then make a recording of yourself playing or singing it.
- Design a Dream Costume.

Dreams and the Australian Aborigines

The Australian Aborigines believe that the world was asleep until the Creator awakened it. The Aborigines have a special name for the Creator: the Rainbow Serpent. They also have a special name for the "forever-within-a-forever" time after the awakening: the Dreamtime.

Dream Art

Try to remember a dream you had recently. Close your eyes and think about what happened in the dream, how you felt, and what the dream meant to you. Now use this space to turn your dream into a work of art. It can be a drawing, a cartoon, a poem, or anything else you can think of.

In the first part of the Dreamtime, the Rainbow Serpent created giant creatures that resemble the people and animals who now live on the earth. The Rainbow Serpent allowed many "sub-creators" to journey throughout the land and leave parts of their spirits or essences behind. When these spirits or essences were later awakened, they became the Australian animals we know today — kangaroos, eels, honey ants, and so on. The journey of the subcreators was called the Dreaming.

Aborigine inventor Eric Willmot explains the Dreaming this way: "A person who says he belongs to the honey-ant dreaming means that his group of people and, perhaps, the honey ants were awakened at some related time and in some related form."*

The Aborigines' theory about the birth of the world is one reason they feel so close to the land. They consider many places sacred because they believe that Dreamtime spirits left their essences there.

The Aborigines, like the Senoi and the Naskapi, are convinced that dreams are much more than images that come to us while we sleep. They see dreams as playing an important part in creation — whether that creation is an entire world, a peaceful society, an idea, or a work of art.

**"We are the music makers,
We are the dreamers
of dreams."**
Arthur O'Shaugnessy

*This information is from Kathy Keeton, "Interview with Eric Willmot," *Omni*, June 1987, page 88.

Beginning Your Dream Journal

Before you can keep a Dream Journal, you have to remember your dreams. Some people claim that they seldom or never dream. In fact, they *do* — they just forget everything about their dreams as soon as they awake.

Dreams fade very quickly. Unless you've had a very dramatic or scary dream, you probably won't be able to recall it if you don't write it down or tell someone about it *immediately*. A Dream Journal is a permanent record of your dreams. It sends a signal to your unconscious mind that you *want* to remember your dreams and *intend* to remember your dreams.

You can actually train yourself to remember your dreams. Try the tips on page 20 — or make up others that work for you.

Writing Your Dream Stories

Think of yourself as the "author" of your dreams. (After all, your dreams are *your* creations.) As you begin recording your dreams, include the same elements a short story writer or play writer would use.

— TITLE. Give each dream a title. It can be short and simple, long and descriptive, serious or silly.

Tips For Remembering Your Dreams

🌙 Keep your Dream Journal and a pencil or pen next to your bed. Every morning, *as soon as you wake up,* write down everything you can recall about your dream or a few key words describing it. Dreams can disappear from your memory in less than five minutes, so don't wait to do this until you've gotten dressed or had breakfast.

🌙 Keep a glass of water next to your bed. Every night, *as soon as you start feeling sleepy,* drink the water and say to yourself, "Tonight I WILL remember my dreams." Repeat this phrase while you are falling asleep. Be sure to say "will remember" instead of "try to remember." (This is called *autosuggestion.* You have probably used it in the past — when you have made yourself wake up at a certain time in the morning by telling yourself to on the night before.)

🌙 Use imaging to "set the stage" for your dreams. As you are falling asleep, picture yourself in a certain place and time. Make up a movie with yourself as the star.

🌙 Keep a record of important or unusual events that happen in your waking life. Try to draw connections between those events and the events that occur in your dreams. This will strengthen the links between your conscious mind and your unconscious mind.

— PLOT. This is the "storyline" of your dream. Describe the events of your dream as if they are happening *right now.* Instead of writing "I ran," write "I am running." Using the present tense helps you keep the sense of being in the middle of your dream.

— SETTING. Describe the time and place of your dream. Are you indoors or outside? Are you in the past, the present, or the future? Are the places you see familiar or strange? Be as specific as you can. If you are walking through a house, what color are the walls? Are there any windows? What rooms are you in? Do you smell anything cooking? Do you hear music?

— PROPS. In a play, the props are the furnishings, costumes, or other objects used to set the mood. Are the rooms in your dream empty or cluttered? Is there a clock, a table, or any other particular piece of furniture? Are you carrying anything?

— CHARACTERS. Who are the main characters in your dream? How old are they? What do they look like? Are they people you know in real life? Try to come up with one word or a short sentence to describe each character in your dream.

— YOUR ROLE IN THE DREAM. Do you make things happen, or do things happen to you? Are you an actor or a watcher? Do you solve any problems? Are you a hero?

— MOOD. Is this a good dream or a bad dream? Does the dream make you feel sad, angry, or confused? Happy, giggly, or excited? Powerful or helpless? Brave or frightened? Be sure to write down your feelings. These can be important clues to what your dreams mean.

If You're Not Quite Ready To Start Writing...

In order to keep a Dream Journal, you have to write down your dreams. If you feel ready to start, skip this section and go straight to the Dream Journal Practice Pages 22 - 23.

If you *don't* feel ready to start, use these techniques to get in the habit of remembering your dreams:

• Keep a tape recorder by your bed and "talk" your dreams into it *as soon as you wake up.*

• Tell your dreams to another person *as soon as you wake up.* (You should know that this is the *least* reliable way to keep a record of your dreams. You can't count on someone else to remember them for you.)

• Keep a pad of blank paper by your bed and draw one or two images from your dreams *as soon as you wake up.* Use markers or crayons if you like to draw in color. Since your dream will fade quickly, you will need to sketch quickly — great practice for drawing class! You may want to write brief notes around or after your sketches.

Dream Journal Practice Pages

Use pages 22 - 23 as practice for starting and keeping your own Dream Journal.

Hints:

• Don't try to figure out what your dreams mean — not yet. We'll get into dream interpretation in the next section. For now, focus on writing down the most important parts of your dreams — what you saw, sensed, heard, did, felt, and so on.

• Date each page. If you're like many people who begin Dream Journals, you may continue recording some or most of your dreams for the rest of your life. And you may go back and reread old Dream Journals from time to time. Dating your dreams can help to remind you of what was happening in your life when you had a particular dream.

• Don't worry about spelling or punctuation or grammar or anything else — just write! It's *your* Dream Journal. Nobody is going to grade it; nobody else even has to see it, unless you choose to share it with someone special. In other words, your Dream Journal is PRIVATE!

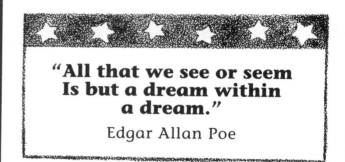

"All that we see or seem Is but a dream within a dream."

Edgar Allan Poe

My Dream

Date: _____ Title: _____

Plot: _____

_____

_____

_____

_____

Setting: _____

_____

_____

Props: _____

_____

_____

_____

Characters: _____

_____

_____

_____

My Role: _____

_____

_____

Mood (My Feelings): _____

_____

_____

My Dream

Date: _____ Title: _____

Plot: _____

_____

_____

_____

Setting: _____

_____

_____

Props: _____

_____

_____

_____

Characters: _____

_____

_____

_____

My Role: _____

_____

_____

Mood (My Feelings): _____

_____

_____

Interpreting Your Dreams

Most Dream Journal keepers aren't satisfied with simply recording their dreams. They also want to know what their dreams *mean*.

Interpreting your dreams helps you to connect them to your waking life. By making these connections, you can figure out what your dreams are trying to tell you. And once you have an idea of what your dreams are trying to tell you, you can use this understanding to fight your fears, solve your problems, and reach your goals. You can use it to get along better with your family and friends, communicate with your parents, and feel better about yourself.

This may seem like a lot to expect of your dreams. But the more you learn about them, the more you will learn about yourself, your emotions, your expectations, your hopes, and your relationships with others.

Important

If you share your dreams with your parents, friends, or teachers, they may add their own thoughts about what your dreams mean. That's okay — as long as you (and they) remember that *you're* the best interpreter of your own dreams. *You're* the only person who *really* knows what your dreams are all about.

Guidelines for Dream Interpretation

One of the best ways to interpret a dream is by asking yourself questions about it and writing down your answers. Of course, you should write down your dream *first* — as soon as you wake up. Later in the day, when you have more time, you can reread your description as a way to refresh your memory. You may find that certain key words bring even more memories rushing back. If you like, you can write these down, too. Remember to keep thinking (and writing) about your dream in the present tense.

Here are some questions to ask yourself about your dream:

"Do certain words or images dominate my dream?"

Do I hear the same words or see the same things more than once? Are certain words or images especially clear or powerful? What do these words or images make me think of?

"Is anything 'wrong' in my dream?"

Is an important object missing from my dream? Or if it is there, is it in the wrong place? Is something happening at the wrong time? Is someone I know in an unexpected place or doing something strange or unusual?

"Have I had this dream before?"

If so, when? Was the dream exactly the same or a little different? Could this dream be related to some continuing situation in my life?

Here are some questions to ask yourself about your waking life:

"Did anything important happen on the day before the dream?"

Was there anything that puzzled me, bothered me, or made me feel happy or hopeful?

"How did I feel on the day before the dream?"

Was I in an especially good mood, an especially bad mood, or just an ordinary mood? Was I excited, worried, energetic, tired, "up" or "down"?

"What did I eat before I went to bed?"

(Remember that what you eat can affect what you dream. Foods that are good for your body are also good for your dreams. If you discover a pattern of junk-food-before-bed, bad-dreams-after, then it's time to make a change!)

Now try to "pull together" your dream and your waking life with this question:

"What do I think my dream is telling me?"

("I don't know" isn't good enough. It may take some effort, but try to come up with an answer or two. There are no "right" or "wrong" answers. There are only *your* answers. When an explanation is right, it will *feel* right to you.)

"Many's the night I've dreamed of cheese — toasted, mostly."

Robert Louis Stevenson

Dream Interpretation Practice Pages

I f you used the Dream Journal Practice Pages, you've already tried recording some of your dreams. Now try figuring out what they mean to you.

Hints:

- Dreams are a rich source of information about you, your life, and your innermost private thoughts. Nothing is too "unimportant" to write about. Record *anything* that occurs to you. A certain word or image might not mean much now, but it could trigger more memories or insights later.

- Watch for patterns. Be sure to note recurring images (images that come into your dreams again and again) and recurring dreams (whole dreams that happen again and again). Often, recurring images and dreams are trying to tell you something special.

- Remember that *you* know the most about your own dreams. *You* are the only person who can really understand them.

- As you form the habit of recording and interpreting your dreams, pay attention to what you're learning about *yourself*. Keeping a Dream Journal is almost like getting to know another you!

My Dream

Date: _____ Title: _____

Plot: _____

_____

_____

_____

Setting: _____

_____

_____

Props: _____

_____

_____

_____

Characters: _____

_____

_____

_____

My Role: _____

_____

_____

Mood (My Feelings): _____

_____

_____

Interpreting My Dream

Important words or images from my dream:

_____

_____

Anything "wrong" in my dream:

_____

_____

If I have had this dream before...
When did I have this dream before?

_____

_____

Here are the ways my dream was the same this time:

_____

_____

Here are the ways my dream was different this time:

_____

_____

Here are some things in my real life that this dream might "connect" to:

_____

_____

What happened on the day before the dream:

_____

_____

How I felt on the day before the dream:

_____

_____

What I ate before I went to bed:

_____

_____

Here is what I think my dream is telling me:

_____

_____

Anything else I want to say or remember or conclude about my dream:

_____

_____

_____

_____

My Dream

Date: _____ Title: _____

Plot: _____

_____

_____

_____

Setting: _____

_____

_____

Props: _____

_____

_____

_____

Characters: _____

_____

_____

_____

My Role: _____

_____

_____

Mood (My Feelings): _____

_____

_____

Interpreting My Dream

Important words or images from my dream:

_____

_____

Anything "wrong" in my dream:

_____

_____

If I have had this dream before...
When did I have this dream before?

_____

_____

Here are the ways my dream was the same this time:

_____

_____

Here are the ways my dream was different this time:

_____

_____

Here are some things in my real life that this dream might "connect" to:

_____

_____

What happened on the day before the dream:

_____

_____

How I felt on the day before the dream:

_____

_____

What I ate before I went to bed:

_____

_____

Here is what I think my dream is telling me:

_____

_____

Anything else I want to say or remember or conclude about my dream:

_____

_____

_____

_____

Dream Symbols

As a member of the human race, you are born, grow up, and grow old. You share the earth with plants, animals, and other people, with mountains and valleys and rivers and oceans.

For as long as humans have lived on the planet, these things have been true.

You have them in common today, in your own life, with all other humans who have lived in the past, who live now, and who will live in the future.

Throughout history, humans have identified common themes and symbols which help them to make sense out of life's changes and events. Carl Jung called these universal images *archetypal symbols*. Archetypal symbols appear over and over again in people's dreams, religions, myths, and fairy tales.

Common Dream Symbols and Their Meanings

☾ **Characters in a dream** may symbolize parts of you which resemble those characters.

☾ **Bad dream characters** may indicate problems or conflicts.

☾ A **house** may symbolize your beliefs or attitudes.

☾ **Water** may symbolize how you feel. For example, if you see water in a dream, is it stormy or calm? Frozen or free-flowing?

☾ **Dead characters** may symbolize parts of you which are becoming less important in your daily life.

☾ **Cars** may symbolize "getting around" in life. They can reflect either your personality or your physical body.

☾ **Roads, paths and highways** may represent choices or decisions. Pay attention to the types of roads you see in your dreams, and compare them. Is one paved? Is another overgrown with weeds? Where does each road seem to lead?

☾ **Stones** (including gemstones, monuments, and memorials) may symbolize eternity. In dreams, a stone may symbolize your inner self — the part of you that lasts forever.

☾ A **circle** may symbolize the whole self (because it is complete and perfect).

☾ A **mirror** can show you another side of yourself.

☾ **Crossing a bridge** may symbolize a change in attitude.

Because of their universal quality, archetypal symbols are a good starting point for making connections between your dreams and your waking life. Over time, people have come up with interpretations and definitions for these symbols. Some of them may relate to your dreams or give you clues to understanding them. But don't be misled by interpretations or definitions that don't seem to fit your dreams or make much sense to you. Think of the Cinderella fairy tale. Like the glass slipper, the right interpretation of a dream symbol will fit *you* and *only* you. Each symbol in your dreams is *yours alone*!

Shedding Light on Your Shadow Self

Dreams can reveal things about you that you wouldn't admit to anyone else. Facing them can help you to understand yourself better and become a better person.

Carl Jung called these things your "shadow." Together they make up your "shadow self." In the *Star Wars* trilogy, the shadow self was called "the Dark Side."

Luke Skywalker's shadow self was personified in Darth Vader. During his training with the Jedi Master Yoda, Luke was forced to crawl through a cave and confront whatever he found there. Of course, he found Darth Vader. When Luke lifted the helmet from Darth Vader's head, he saw his own face! Before he could harness the full power of "the Force" — the good side of himself — Luke had to accept that the Dark Side also existed in him. Only then could he understand and use his power for good instead of evil.

Often, the qualities you fear or dislike in others are parts of your own shadow self. You may wonder how you can fight against these qualities. Luckily, the lesson of the shadow self is a simple one: By admitting to yourself that you are not perfect, you automatically become more perfect and powerful. Of course, you must also admit to your many wonderful qualities! The trick here is to paint an honest picture of yourself — not too glowing, and not too grim. Take a realistic view of yourself, learn to like yourself just the way you are, and the Dark Side of *your* shadow self will have less power in your life.

A popular 1940s radio show began with the line: "Who knows what evil lurks in the hearts of men? The Shadow knows!" In your dreams, you can act out things you never would "dream" of doing in real life. Dreams keep your shadow self from getting in the way of your waking thoughts and feelings. They help you to "own" your feelings, good and bad, and to face your faults and shortcomings. And this makes you a better, stronger person.

The depth of a shadow depends upon the object that is casting the shadow. Try this Shadow Experiment:

1. Hold a piece of clear plastic food wrap in front of the afternoon sun and observe the shadow it casts.

2. Do the same thing with a piece of waxed paper.

3. Do the same thing with a piece of paper cut from a brown paper bag.

What is different about the shadows cast by these three types of wrappings? Which casts the deepest, darkest shadow? Does this experiment tell you anything about shadow and substance? (What is a "person of substance" like?) Can you see any relation between the kind of person you are and your shadow self? (Maybe "deeper" people have stronger shadow selves.)

The depth of a shadow also depends on how much light there is and where it is located. There are no shadows in complete darkness. A person who casts no shadow may be thought of as being "in the dark" or unaware of events going on around him or her. Maybe that's why Peter Pan wanted his shadow back!

There are also no shadows in complete light. The point here is that reality is made up of a combination of light and dark, good and bad. The balance between the two is what results in a balanced life.

Shadow Sayings

Our language is full of references to shadows. Here are a few sayings you may have heard:

- He's afraid of his own shadow!

- She's a shadow of her former self.

- The detective shadowed the suspect.

What do these sayings mean to you? Can you think of any more shadow sayings?

Dream Associations

Sometimes the images or symbols you see in your dreams can stand for words and their meanings. Importantly, dreams often use *puns* to get their message across. For example, shoes could indicate your underSTANDing of something. Or piles of books in your home could indicate HOMEwork.

Here are some possible interpretations that might apply to dreaming about a ship:

- "My SHIP is coming in." (Something good is about to happen.)

- "RelationSHIP." (Are you having any trouble in a relationship?)

- "FriendSHIP." (Think about your friendships. Is anything special or important going on?)

- "We're all in the same BOAT." (Have you been sharing your problems or thoughts with anyone lately?)

- "It's time to SHIP out!" (Is there a situation you need to get out of or change?)

My Shadow Self

Use this space to describe or draw your shadow self. Then think about what this description or drawing tells you about yourself.

People you have read or heard about often appear in your dreams because their first or last names stand for something else. What could it mean if you saw these people in your dreams? (Forget about their celebrity status or the way they look. Focus on their names only.)

- Michael J. Fox
- Bob Hope
- Tom Cruise
- Sting
- Madonna
- the Beatles
- Carrie Fisher

Making associations is a good way to understand what a dream is trying to tell you. It's easy, and it's fun! Here's how to do it:

1. Choose an important object or character from your dream.

2. Draw the object or the character (or write the character's name) in the center of a sheet of paper.

3. Draw several lines extending out from the drawing or name.

4. At the end of each line, write down something you associate with the object or character.

5. Note any possible puns or plays on words, if they occur to you.

For example, let's say that you have a dream about Santa Claus. Below are some of the associations you might make. Some are positive; some are negative. All of them are okay.

What other associations can *you* make? For example, do you have friends named Chris or Nick? Or memories from when you were little and sat on Santa's lap yourself?

Association is a "dream investigation" technique. No association you come up with is too silly or far-fetched to write down. Your unconscious mind knows things that your waking mind doesn't easily recognize. When you "let yourself go" while making associations, you sometimes reach your unconscious mind. One of the associations you make could hold the key to understanding your dream.

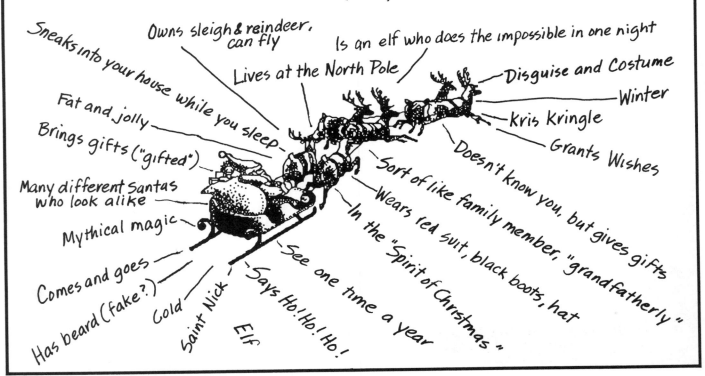

Owns sleigh & reindeer, can fly
Sneaks into your house while you sleep
Is an elf who does the impossible in one night
Lives at the North Pole
Disguise and Costume
Winter
Fat and jolly
Kris Kringle
Brings gifts ("gifted")
Grants Wishes
Doesn't know you, but gives gifts
Sort of like family member, "grandfatherly"
Many different Santas who look alike
Wears red suit, black boots, hat
Mythical magic
In the "Spirit of Christmas"
Comes and goes
See one time a year
Has beard (fake?)
Cold
Saint Nick
Says Ho! Ho! Ho!
Elf

34

My Dream Associations

Use this space to make your own dream associations.

Making a Dream Dictionary

The more you record and interpret your dreams, the more you will notice that certain colors, words, images, symbols, and associations are repeated.

A Dream Dictionary can help you to keep track of these and what you think they mean. Because what you dream and your interpretations of what you dream are both very personal, you won't find a Dream Dictionary in a store. You'll have to make your own!

My Dream Dictionary

Use this space to record the colors, words, images, symbols, and associations that keep coming up in your dreams. Write what you think each one means in your personal "dream vocabulary."

Traveling The Hero Path

Every person must travel the path from childhood innocence to adult maturity and independence. You follow that path again and again — in your dreams. Your dream self is the hero or heroine of thrilling and dangerous adventures! These heroic adventures can lead you to a greater understanding of yourself.

The "hero path" is the stuff of legend and literature. Every human civilization has its stories and songs of heroes. The Greek poet Homer turned the heroic adventures of Ulysses into his epic, the *Odyssey*. The exploits of King Arthur and his Knights of the Round Table continue to inspire poetry, novels, and art. Whether naive, foolhardy, or frightened, heroes and heroines always overcome their shortcomings for the greater good of humankind.

Seven basic elements are found in the heroic adventure. When any of these elements appear in your dream adventures, carefully think about what they might mean. Your dream journeys on the hero path are telling you something important about yourself and the progress you are making toward maturity and independence.

1. **Humble birth.** Heroes generally come from ordinary environments. Could this be because all humans start life in the same way, no matter what riches or fame they may gain in later life?

2. **Early proof of super-ability.** Heroes can perform amazing deeds even when very young. Likewise, humans learn an incredible amount in the first two years of life.

3. **A rapid rise to power.** Because of their awesome abilities, people trust their heroes with large responsibilities. The fate of thousands often depends upon one heroic person!

4. **The appearance of a helper or "guardian."** King Arthur's wizard advisor, Merlin, and Luke Skywalker's teacher, Ben Kenobi, are heroic guardians. The helper symbolizes the greater self from which the ordinary self can draw strength and guidance. Helper/guardian figures may show up in dreams as wise old men or wise old women.

5. **The presence of obstacles to overcoming the forces of evil.** These obstacles — whether dragons, witches, or an evil emperor — represent the shadow self. The key to victory lies in recognizing and understanding the secret shadow power of the enemy.

6. **A setback or "fall" due to overconfidence.** Do you remember the Greek myth of the fall of Icarus? When he escaped from the Minotaur's palace wearing wings made by his father, Icarus flew too near the sun. The wax holding his wings together melted, and Icarus fell to his death in the ocean.

   Falling in a dream sometimes means that you are reaching beyond what you know you can do. However, you should try to get up again. Even in dreams, you can learn by taking risks. (See pages 45 - 46 to find out how the Senoi change falling dreams into flying dreams.)

7. **Death through heroic sacrifice or betrayal.** A heroic death is a symbol of growing up. The "old" self is being replaced by an independent, mature self. This can be a very positive dream, showing growth and new understanding.

"Even in dreams good works are not wasted."
Pedro Calderón de la Barca

Heroic Adventurers in Literature

You may already "know" some of these heroes. And you may want to "meet" those you don't already know. The best place to meet them is at the library!

- **Frodo** — The hobbit hero of J.R.R. Tolkien's *The Lord of the Rings* trilogy.

- **Beowulf** — The courageous hero of an epic Anglo-Saxon poem composed about 700 A.D.

- **Ulysses** — The Trojan War hero of Homer's *Odyssey*. (There are many, many heroes in Greek and Roman mythology. Ask your librarian to direct you toward books about them that are fun and interesting to read.)

- **Wart** — The young King Arthur of the Disney movie, "The Sword in the Stone." To find out more about King Arthur as a boy, read T. H. White's *The Once and Future King.*

- **Charlotte** — The clever, loving spider of E. B. White's *Charlotte's Web.*

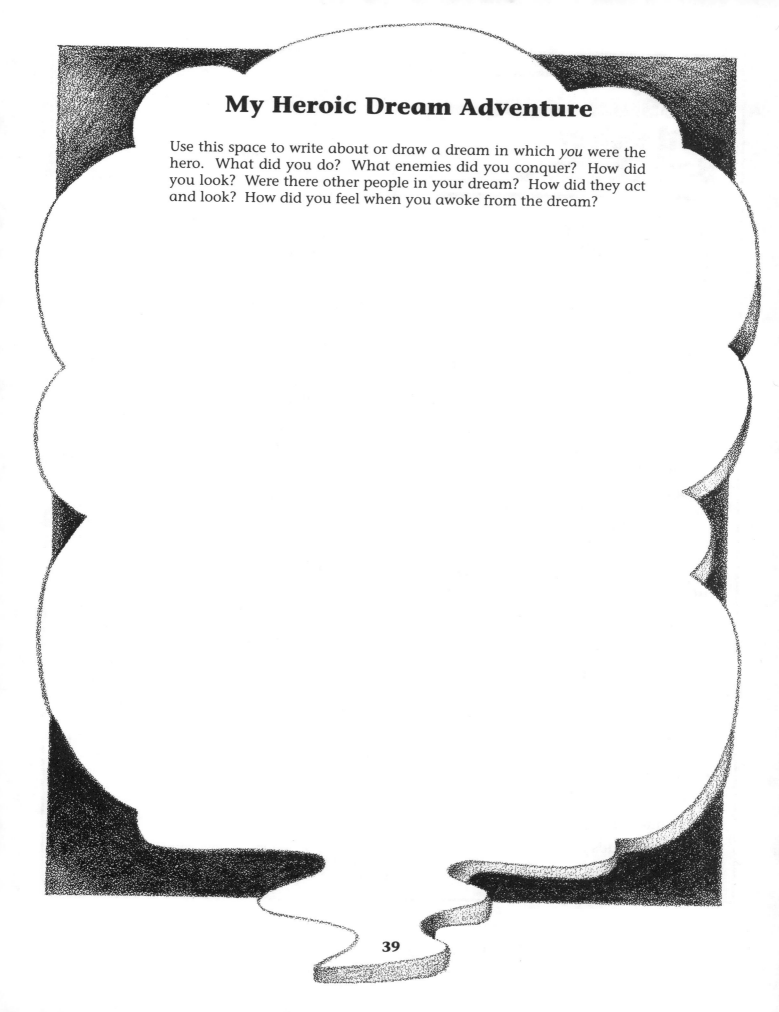

My Heroic Dream Adventure

Use this space to write about or draw a dream in which *you* were the hero. What did you do? What enemies did you conquer? How did you look? Were there other people in your dream? How did they act and look? How did you feel when you awoke from the dream?

Missing Class and Other Bad Dreams

It is the end of May. Jeremy is supposed to finish fifth grade in two weeks. One night he dreams that he never went to earth sciences lab. He always went to study hall instead. There is no way he can make up the work now. He won't pass — he'll have to repeat fifth grade!

Have you ever had a dream like Jeremy's? If so, you're not alone. Thousands of people have reported some variation of this particular dream. Psychologists believe that the "missing a class or examination" dream reflects feelings of inadequacy or "not measuring up" to expectations.

Of course, Jeremy's dream is not realistic. In real life, if he had gone to study hall instead of earth sciences lab, the study hall teacher would have checked attendance and realized that Jeremy was supposed to be somewhere else. And the earth sciences lab teacher would have reported Jeremy's continued absence from class. Jeremy might have missed a day or two of the lab — but not the entire year!

Have you ever had bad dreams about any of these subjects?

- Arrivals or departures
- Journeys
- Flying
- Falling
- Dangerous crossings
- Lonely roads
- Losing money, gold, or jewels
- Being chased or attacked
- Being oddly dressed — or even naked — in school, in the street, in a store, or some other public place
- Missing an exam or another important school event

Because bad dreams seem so real and so personal, you may feel sometimes as if you're the only person who has them. In fact, many common dreams — especially the ones about being chased or falling — are the stuff of nightmares for both children *and* adults.

Interestingly, people tend to remember bad dreams more often than good dreams. When Dr. Patricia Garfield did a study of children's dreams, she found that 158 of the 288 dreams they reported — or 55 percent — were bad dreams.*

Nobody knows for sure why bad dreams are more memorable than good dreams. Maybe it's because they're more dramatic or exciting. Or maybe it's because people often wake up in the middle of bad dreams or immediately after them, and the dreams stay fresher in their minds as a result. Or maybe there's a message that your subconscious *really* wants to get through to you, so it uses bad dreams as a way to make sure that you'll remember it.

Why do *you* think you remember your bad dreams? Why do you think you *have* bad dreams?

Which memories from your waking life are the most vivid — good ones, or bad ones? What does this tell you about how the mind works?

* This information is from Patricia Garfield, *Your Child's Dreams* (New York: Ballantine Books, 1984), pages 54-55.

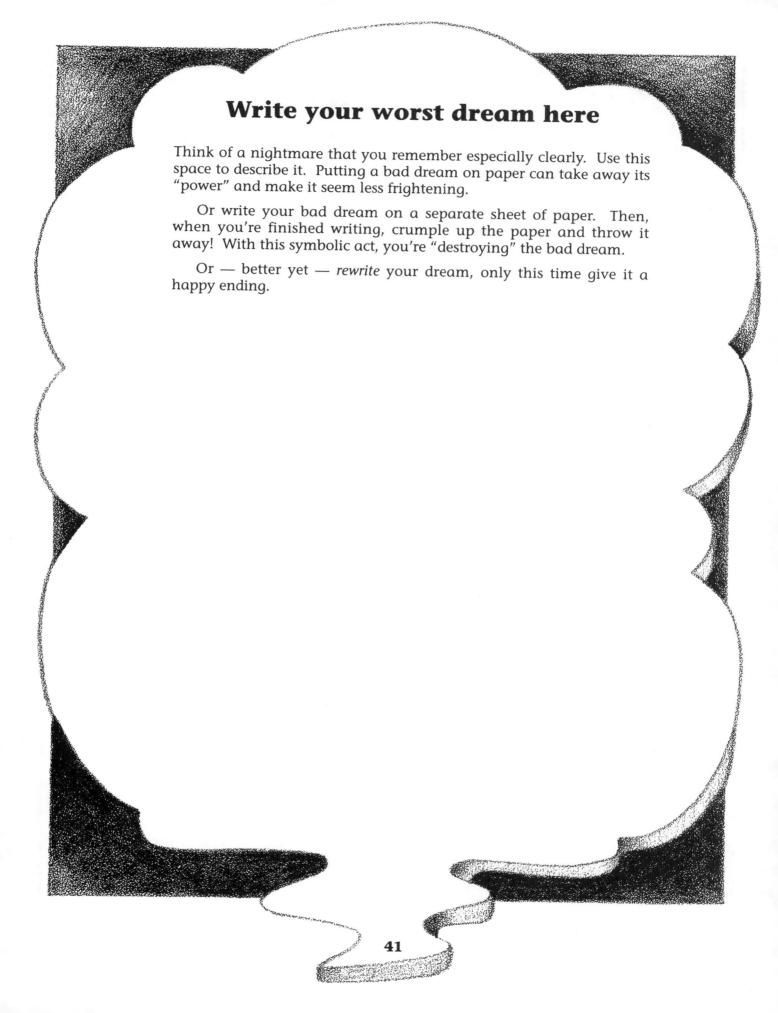

Write your worst dream here

Think of a nightmare that you remember especially clearly. Use this space to describe it. Putting a bad dream on paper can take away its "power" and make it seem less frightening.

Or write your bad dream on a separate sheet of paper. Then, when you're finished writing, crumple up the paper and throw it away! With this symbolic act, you're "destroying" the bad dream.

Or — better yet — *rewrite* your dream, only this time give it a happy ending.

Have you ever had bad dreams about being chased by any of these? Can you relate these common "dream villains" to something you have recently read, seen, or heard?

- A dragon
- A tall, square-headed monster
- A lord who lives in a castle built of skulls
- A snake
- A cold-hearted queen
- A crocodile
- A vampire

Flying and Other Good Dreams

The good dreams you remember are usually very, very good. The exuberant feeling of a wonderful dream spills over into your waking life for hours or even days.

Of all the good dreams people remember, the flying dream is common to most civilizations of the world. Long before Wilbur and Orville Wright made their famous flight at Kitty Hawk, humans dreamed (and daydreamed) about flying. Renaissance artist Leonardo da Vinci tried to invent a flying machine. (He also painted the "Mona Lisa," which you may have seen pictures of or heard about.)

Although we now have jets and spaceships, we can still fly without machines — in our dreams. And what wondrous flights we have! Like Superman, we roam the universe. Flying represents the freedom and power to do anything.

Not everyone is lucky enough to have flying dreams. Sigmund Freud, who spent his life studying people's dreams, said that he never experienced one.

What about you?

**"In dreaming,
The clouds methought
would open and
show riches
Ready to drop upon me;
that, when I wak'd
I cried to dream again."**

—William Shakespeare,
The Tempest

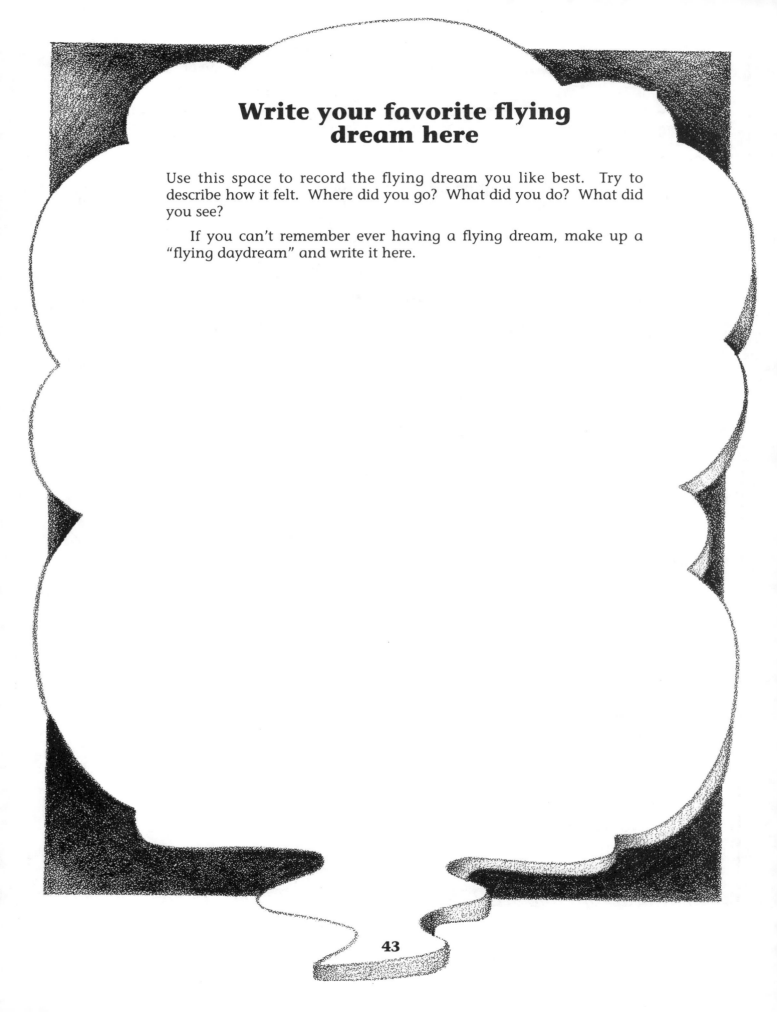

Write your favorite flying dream here

Use this space to record the flying dream you like best. Try to describe how it felt. Where did you go? What did you do? What did you see?

If you can't remember ever having a flying dream, make up a "flying daydream" and write it here.

43

How To Direct Your Dreams

Cathy doesn't have nightmares anymore. When she was seven, she dreamed she was falling into a well. She says, "I remember thinking, I *hate this and I know it's just a dream,* so I woke up. When I'm having a bad dream now, I say to myself, 'If you don't like it, wake up!'"

Cathy has learned how to direct her dreams. She has learned to change what happens in her dreams by thinking differently.

You may not want to "turn off" your dream like Cathy did, but you, too, can direct your dreams. And you don't need a director's chair or Hollywood experience. Instead, try these Dream Directing Techniques.

Dream Directing Techniques

★ Call on dream friends

The next time bad characters invade your dream, face them yourself or call on your "dream friends" for help.

Dream friends are fantasy beings — people or animals you trust. You might want to think of your family dog, your best friend, or your older brother or sister as your special dream ally. Or maybe you can invent your own dream superhero or heroine. Knowing that help is on the way really does make nightmares seem less frightening.

★ Imagine what your favorite hero would do

Think of a favorite hero or heroine in literature or the movies. How did he or she conquer villains? Dorothy poured a bucket of water on the Wicked Witch of the West. Max, the hero of Maurice Sendak's *Where the Wild Things Are,* ruled the wild things "with the magic trick of staring into all their yellow eyes without blinking once." What could *you* do?

★ Turn to real life

You may not be able to control your unconscious mind, but you can influence it by what you put into your conscious mind. For example, if you frequently dream about fires, you could lead a class project on fire prevention. Maybe what you learn will help you put out your next dream fire.

★ Give your dream a new ending

"Redream" your dream while you're awake. Write or draw a new ending — one that turns out the way *you* want it to. Turn your bad dream into a good dream.*

* This suggestion is from Patricia Garfield, *Your Child's Dreams* (New York: Ballantine Books, 1984), pages 283-288.

Lucid Dreaming

Have you ever been awake *inside* a dream, yet continued to dream? If so, you have naturally experienced a technique that can take other people months or years to master.

The state of being awake within a dream is called *lucid dreaming*. Instead of "turning off" a bad dream, a lucid dreamer can consciously choose to stay in the dream and change its direction.

Dr. Stephen LaBerge, who has spent several years studying lucid dreaming with volunteers at the Stanford University Sleep Research Center, says that he had his first lucid dream when he was five. In his dream, he thought he was going to drown. But once he realized that the water was dream-water, he knew that he could not drown. Instead, without the aid of scuba gear, he swam on to further adventures beneath the waves.*

Lucid dreams allow you to apply things you have learned in your waking life to your dreams — and vice versa. LaBerge believes that you can train yourself to have lucid dreams. The first step, he says, is to recall your dreams — just as you are learning to do in this book. Recalling your dreams helps your mind to recognize when you are having a dream.

Many of LaBerge's volunteers have learned to have lucid dreams by using the following technique: Count to yourself as you fall asleep. After each number, say "I'm dreaming." You are reminding yourself to dream. Eventually, you will be dreaming!**

Are You an Oneironaut?

Stephen LaBerge calls the people who volunteer for his lucid dream experiments *oneironauts* (pronounced OH-NYE-ROH-NOTS). He says that this word, which comes from the Greek word for "dream," means "explorers of the mind."

All dreamers — not just lucid dreamers — are oneironauts. And that includes you!

How To Turn Falling Into Flying

Falling dreams often represent your worries or fears. The Senoi have a special way of dealing with falling dreams. They tell their children that falling

* This story is from Anne Fadiman, "Stephen LaBerge: The Doctor of Dreams," *Life*, November 1986, pages 19-20.

** This technique is from Stephen LaBerge, *Lucid Dreaming* (New York: Ballantine Books, 1986), page 149.

dreams are a direct path to the spirit world. They advise them to relax, enjoy themselves, and fall toward the thing that is making them fall. They believe that this thing (whatever it is) is a source of power.

When the children accept this power and try to lean toward it, they are able to turn their falling dreams into flying dreams. Instead of being out of control, the dreamers are in charge!

Once they are flying, the children are told, they should continue flying to a place where they will meet dream people (good spirits) who have something of value for them. Afterward, the children must turn their dreams into poems, songs, dances, or ideas to share with the tribe.

See if you can make this happen in your own dreams. Flying is much more fun than falling! Then turn your dream into a poem, song, dance, or idea to share with your family or friends.

How To Use Your Daydreams To Make Your Real Dreams Come True

You never know when a daydream will come along and sweep you away. One day in early spring, you happen to glance out the window. The moment you see the sky, a thought strikes you. The moment becomes two moments, and the thought becomes two thoughts. Soon you are immersed in your daydream.

Don't confuse daydreaming with lucid dreaming. Lucid dreaming occurs only when you are asleep. Daydreaming is an "awake" activity. You daydream on purpose because you like to imagine the future or remember the past. In a daydream, anything is possible!

Why don't you take a daydream trip right now? Relax. Breathe deeply. Imagine yourself floating off to your favorite place. Smell the smells, see the sights, hear the sounds. How do you feel?

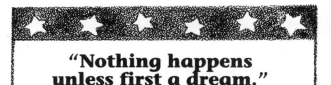

"Nothing happens unless first a dream."
Edgar Cayce

You can use your daydreams to help make your *real* dreams come true. Here's how:

1. Get a large piece of posterboard in your favorite color. Paste a picture of yourself in the center.

2. Write these words on the posterboard: "Where I Am Going From Where I Am."

3. Find pictures in magazines or newspapers that illustrate your personal goals in life. Paste them around your picture.

4. Hang your Daydream Collage in a place where you will see it often.

Putting your daydreams in concrete form reminds you to work toward your goals. Seeing yourself surrounded by pictures of your goals makes them look achievable. Knowing your goals helps you recognize opportunities to reach them. Instead of relying on luck, you become more aware and observant.

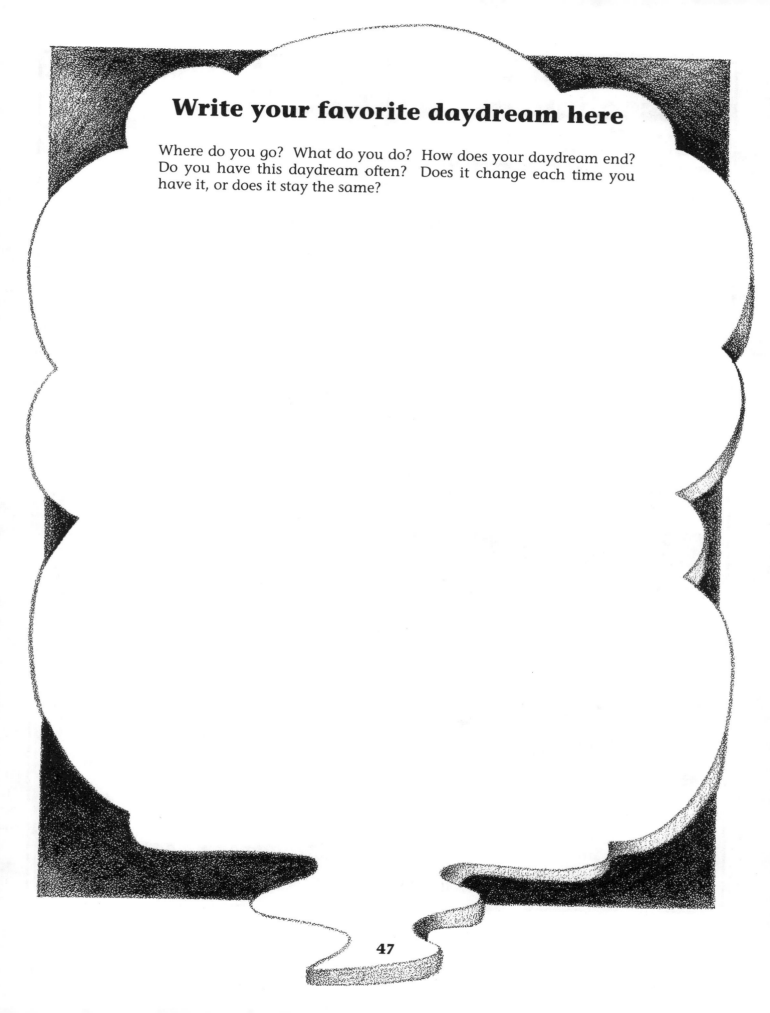

Write your favorite daydream here

Where do you go? What do you do? How does your daydream end?
Do you have this daydream often? Does it change each time you
have it, or does it stay the same?

Dissecting Your Dreams

Now that you've had practice recording and interpreting your dreams — and maybe even directing some of them — you're *almost* ready to start keeping your Dream Journal.

Here's one more technique to help you figure out what your dreams mean to you.

Instead of asking yourself, "What does my dream mean?", try "dissecting" your dream and breaking it up into smaller parts. Then make up a question about just one of those parts. This question shouldn't have a "yes" or "no" answer. It should have several possible answers. One of the answers may hold the key to the "whole" meaning of your dream.

> **"So I awoke, and behold it was a dream."**
>
> John Bunyan

Kids Speak Out About Their Dreams

Before you begin dissecting your own dreams, you can try this technique on dreams other children have had. Pages 49 - 55

contain descriptions of several dreams, possible interpretations, and "part questions" that will get you thinking about how to do this for yourself.

As you read each dream, decide if you agree with the interpretation. Or do you think the dream means something else? Can you come up with other "part questions" that you would have liked to ask the dreamers about their dreams?

Share Your Dreams!

We would like to hear about *your* dreams. When you start keeping your Dream Journal, pick out one or two you would like to share. Make copies and send them to:

Jonni Kincher
DREAMS
c/o Free Spirit Publishing
400 First Avenue North
Suite 616
Minneapolis, MN 55401-1730

Be sure to date your dream and include your name, your address, and your age at the time you had the dream.

Monstrous Candy Bar by Joseph, 10

I am looking out the window of my two-story house. A giant Hershey bar is on the front lawn. It is as big as my whole front lawn. It seems like it would be too much to ever eat. I do not like it.

WHAT I THINK MY DREAM MEANS: You can have too much of a good thing or too much to handle. I have been doing so well in school and my other activities that it just seems like too much sometimes.

Why do you think Joseph dreamed of a chocolate bar? (Why chocolate and not some other kind?)

_____

_____

_____

_____

Olympic Jealousy by Kristina, 11

I am on the playground, playing on the bars. I am better than good. I am as good as someone who is in the Olympics. At first it is fun and then I become embarrassed because I am so much better than all of the other kids. They begin to hate me for being better.

WHAT I THINK MY DREAM MEANS: I think I am scared of losing friends if I do my very best.

What does this dream say about Kristina's definition of the word "friend"?

_____

_____

_____

_____

Dracula Movie Comes Alive by Eric, 8

My parents leave me and my two brothers at the movie while they go across the street to shop at the K-Mart. The movie is about Dracula. Dracula comes out of the movie screen and tries to get us. We run. I run up the stairs by the side of the screen. I am running up the stairs and suddenly Dracula is not chasing me, he is at the top of the stairs! Then my parents pick us all up.

WHAT I THINK MY DREAM MEANS: When I run from something, it will just be waiting for me at the top of the stairs.

Do you think Eric would really have found Dracula if he had gone to the top of the stairs?

_____

_____

_____

_____

Sailing on a Day Full of Horror by Autumn, 9

I am in a boat and there is a shark attack. I am one of the victims.
(I watched a "Jaws" movie the night before this dream.)

    WHAT I THINK MY DREAM MEANS: Don't swim in shark-infested
(or dangerous) waters.

*Why did Autumn and her sailing companions get into a situation they
knew was dangerous?*

_____

_____

_____

_____

A Trip to Space by Amber, 9

I go to the planet Pluto. On the planet, they are having dog races. The dogs look like Pluto from Disneyland. The dog handlers are from other planets and I am an observer.

WHAT I THINK MY DREAM MEANS: I had been talking about Disneyland the day before. Maybe this dream was about the fun I would have if I went there.

Why did Amber have to go to such a distant and exotic place to see something as ordinary as a dog race?

_____

_____

_____

_____

A War Dream by Kirsten, 10

I am a leader, and the characters in my dream are like me a little bit. In real life, the characters are my friends, but they are not my friends in my dream. My dog is doing flips off of the doghouse.

WHAT I THINK MY DREAM MEANS: I would like to be the leader, but some of my friends don't want me to be a leader.

Why do you think Kirsten's dog is doing flips off the doghouse?

_____

_____

_____

_____

Running from Monsters by Travis, 7

I am running away from these wild monsters. They just keep chasing me and chasing me. Then I come to the edge of a cliff. I stop and turn around to look at them. When I look at them, they all disappear!

WHAT I THINK MY DREAM MEANS: When you turn around and face your problems, they will disappear. But if you try to run away from them, they will just keep following you.

What do you think would have happened to Travis if he had kept on running?

More Dreamers and Their Dreams

All cultures have stories about dreamers and their dreams. As you add to your Dream Journal, you may want to visit the library to learn about other dreamers.

To get you started, here is a Chinese tale about two dreamers and their dreams.*

In the state of Chou lived the head of the Yin clan. His servants worked hard from dawn until dark. The head of the clan thought little about his servants and their condition. But he thought much about his possessions and his power.

One of the oldest of the servants worked extremely hard. Each day, his body and spirit grew older and weaker. At night, exhausted, he slept soundly. In his sleep he dreamed that he was the king of the realm, with great power and wealth. His every desire was met. There was no limit on what he could do or have. Every morning, when he awoke from his dream, he went back to his work as a servant.

When friends spoke to the servant about his hard life, the old man would always reply, "Man lives a hundred years, half in days, half in nights. By day I am a lowly servant with a heavy burden on my shoulders. But at night I have powers that few men ever dream of having. With one-half so pleasant, what have I to complain of?"

The clan head was also weary when he went to sleep at night. But his dreams were very different. He was not a ruler, but a lowly servant, rushing and carrying the weight of the world on his shoulders. He was weak and was beaten regularly with a stick. Each night he had this dream, and it troubled his sleep greatly.

He told his dream to a wise man who gave him good advice. The wise man told him that his dream represented the cycle of good and bad fortune. "You cannot have both your dream and your waking life the same," the wise man said.

The head of the Yin clan thought about the wise man's words. He gave his servants less work and began to treat them better. He started to do more for himself. He reduced his own worries. His heart became lighter and his dreams more pleasant. He rested well and awoke feeling refreshed each day. He became a wiser and better ruler.

* This folk tale has been adapted from "Dreams" by Lieh Tzu, in *Chinese Fairy Tales and Fantasies*, translated and edited by Moss Roberts (New York: Pantheon Books, 1979), pages 216 - 217.

Dear Servants, Please take the day off today. Signed The Head of the Yin Clan

Dream Discoveries

Your dreams not only lead you to discoveries about yourself. They can also lead you to discoveries that may change the world!

Throughout history, musicians, poets, artists, scientists, philosophers, and inventors have used their dreams as inspiration and sources for important ideas. Thomas Edison once said: "I never created anything, my dreams did."

In dreams, you allow yourself to see what you already know but don't recognize when you are awake. The different state of mind you enter during sleep, as shown by brain wave patterns, seems to provide a framework for increased creativity and problem-solving ability. As the dream discoveries of many famous people prove, your dreams may provide a legacy for future generations.

Three Famous Dreams

★ Physicist **Niels Bohr** (1885-1962) had a dream in which he saw himself on a sun of burning gas. Planets whistled as they rushed past him in their revolutions around the sun. These dream planets were attached to the sun by thin filaments. Suddenly the burning gas cooled and solidified. The sun and planets crumbled away. When Bohr awoke, he realized that he had seen the model of an atom. His dream marked the beginning of modern atomic theory.

★ Inventor **Elias Howe** (1819-1867) dreamed that he was captured by savages who dragged him before their king. The king sentenced Howe to death unless he could produce a machine that could sew. He gave Howe 24 hours to come up with the machine. Howe failed to meet the deadline. As the spears of the savages started to fall on him, he noticed the spears all had eye-shaped holes in their tips. On the basis of that discovery, Howe invented the first sewing machine.

★ Novelist **Robert Louis Stevenson** (1850-1894) dreamed about a criminal who drank a potion to change his appearance. This led him to write *The Strange Case of Dr. Jekyll and Mr. Hyde,* a classic story about the inner battle between good and evil.

Goethe, Voltaire, Dante, Edgar Allen Poe, Frank Lloyd Wright, Mozart, and many other creative people also claimed that dreams inspired their creations. In his autobiography, Robert Louis Stevenson said that he fought off nightmares by imagining wonderful stories as he drifted off to sleep. He found that his dreams often changed his original ideas into stories he could later write down and sell. He called his dreams his "Brownies."

If your dreams seem to be telling you to create something, then try it! Sometimes dreams can help you to put things you already know into a new perspective. That new perspective may be just what you need to complete an unfinished project, invent something entirely new, or write the paper that's due on Friday.

Or maybe a dream makes you feel so wonderful that you just have to write, dance or sing. Do it! Make up your dance, write your poem, or sing your song into a tape recorder. The action inspired by your dream lets you share your joy and vision with other people.

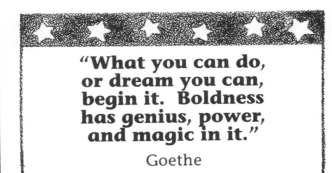

"What you can do, or dream you can, begin it. Boldness has genius, power, and magic in it."

Goethe

Ready...Set...Go!

You've just begun to learn how to use the creativity of your dreams — creativity that springs from your waking mind.

You've just begun to learn how to transfer dream knowledge to your waking life — knowledge that can boost your self-confidence, solve your problems, and help you reach your goals.

Don't stop now! Instead, start your Dream Journal. The next part of this book is waiting to catch and hold your dreams.

Dreams really *can* help you in many ways. They help the Senoi live in peace, and they can help you discover how to use the power you have *within yourself* to live a better, more peaceful, and healthier life.

Dreams can help by keeping you in touch with your own fears, hopes, and concerns. Dreams can help you share those feelings with your parents, brothers, sisters, teachers, and friends. (Sometimes it's easier to talk about a dream character's feelings and ideas than it is to talk about yourself.) Dreams can help open the door to understanding others, too, if you can learn to listen to their dreams with an open mind.

Sometimes dreams can help by warning you about your behavior. One boy realized that he was reading too many comic books when he noticed that comic book themes were taking over his dreams. Another decided that he was playing too many video games when his dreams placed him *inside* a video game machine!

Dreams can help you create stories, songs, plays, dances, and inventions. They can help you by giving you a chance to experience adventures that you might otherwise never have. These adventures can point the way toward solutions to problems in your waking life. They can even help you discover real problems that need solving.

Dreams can help you improve your thinking skills as you work to interpret their puns and hidden meanings. They can even help you eat right, if you pay attention to how what you eat affects what you dream.

Most of all, dreams can help you to be the explorer you were meant to be! When you began your Dream Journal, you became a true oneironaut — an explorer of the mind. The longer you keep your Dream Journal, the more you will learn about the mind.

What you dream at night, and what you do during the day with your dreams, might even help the whole world one day.

Sleep on it!

"To all, to each, a fair good-night,
And pleasing dreams, and slumbers light!"
Sir Walter Scott

Part 2

YOUR DREAM JOURNAL

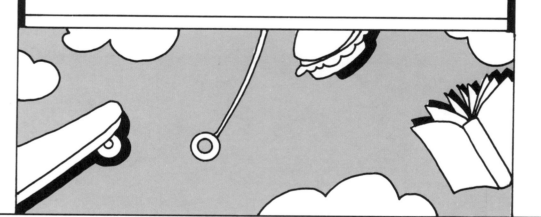

About Your Dream Journal

Use these pages to start your first Dream Journal. We have left them blank on purpose so you can record and interpret your dreams in whatever ways work best for you.

Be sure to try many different ways of "dream journaling." Here are the pages where you can find the ideas you learned about in this book:

Or invent your own ways of "dream journaling." Anything you decide to do is okay. *You* are the dreamer; your dreams belong to *you*. Record them however you want. Interpret them in whatever way feels best and most true to you. Decide for yourself what the images and symbols mean. Only *you* can decide what your dreams are trying to tell you.

"Meet me in Dreamland, sweet dreamy Dreamland, There let my dreams come true."

Beth Slater Whitson

My Dream

Date: _____ Title: _____

Interpreting
My Dream

My Dream

Date: _____ Title: _____

Interpreting
My Dream

My Dream

Date: _____ Title: _____

Interpreting
My Dream

My Dream

Date: _____ Title: _____

Interpreting
My Dream

My Dream

Date: _____ Title: _____

Interpreting
My Dream

My Dream

Date: _____ Title: _____

Interpreting
My Dream

My Dream

Date: _____ Title: _____

Interpreting
My Dream

How To Make Your Own Dream Journal

When you run out of "dream journaling" space in this book, it's time to make your own Dream Journal!

You will need:

- 6 pieces of 8 1/2" x 11" white paper
- 2 pieces of 4 3/8" x 5 5/8" non-corrugated cardboard for covers
- A roll of 1/2" masking tape
- A needle and heavy thread or yarn
- Clear tape
- Rubber cement or glue
- Scissors or a paper cutter
- An 11" x 14" piece of wrapping paper, wallpaper, or fabric for the cover

Here's what to do:

1. Fold the pieces of white paper in half. Lay them on top of one another so the folds line up.

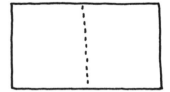

2. With a needle or paper punch, make four holes 1/2" apart along the fold line.

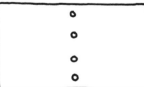

3. Sew the pages together along the fold line with a needle and heavy thread or yarn. Tape the ends of the thread to the back with clear tape. You have now made a 24-page "book."

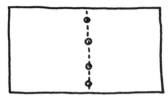

4. Close your book.

5. Place one piece of cardboard on the front of the book and the other on the back. Tape the panels in place at the spine using masking tape. Remove the book and set it aside.

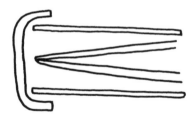

6. Place the taped-together cardboard covers tape-side down on the wrapping paper, wallpaper, or fabric. Make sure that a border shows all around.

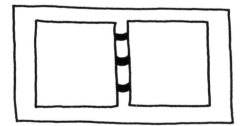

7. Fold in all four corners.

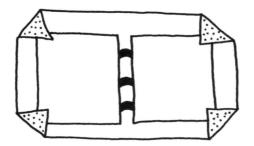

8. Fold in the edges as if you were wrapping a package. Smooth and glue them with rubber cement or glue.

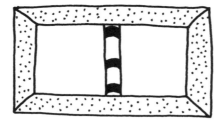

9. Line up your book tape-side down with the center spine of the cover. Glue the front and back pages to the insides of the cover. This will hold the pages securely inside.

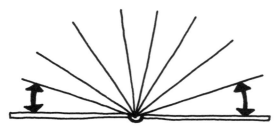

10. Keep your Dream Journal beside your bed, and write in it *every* morning as soon as you wake up.

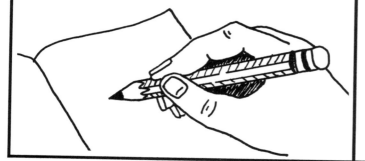

More Ways To Make A Dream Journal

◖ Fill a 3-ring notebook with plenty of blank pages.

◖ Fill a 3-ring notebook with photocopies of the Dream Journal pages in this book.

◖ Put a pad of blank paper in a clipboard. Each morning, record your dream on a sheet of blank paper, then tear it off the pad and store it in a folder.

Bibliography

Books

Delaney, Gayle. *Living Your Dreams.* New York: Harper & Row, Publishers, Inc., 1979.

Evans, Christopher. *Landscapes of the Night: How and Why We Dream.* Edited and completed by Peter Evans. New York: The Viking Press, 1984.

Faraday, Ann. *The Dream Game.* New York: Harper & Row, Publishers, Inc., 1974.

Faraday, Ann. *Dream Power.* New York: Coward, McCann & Geoghegan, Inc., 1972.

Freud, Sigmund. *The Interpretation of Dreams.* New York: Random House, Inc., 1938.

Garfield, Patricia. *Creative Dreaming.* New York: Ballantine Books, 1976. Original copyright held by Simon and Schuster, New York, 1974.

Garfield, Patricia. *Your Child's Dreams.* New York: Ballantine Books, 1984.

Jung, Carl G. *Man and His Symbols.* Doubleday & Co., Inc. , 1964. Original copyright held by Aldus Books, Ltd., London, 1964.

LaBerge, Stephen. *Lucid Dreaming.* New York: Ballantine Books, 1986. Published by arrangement with Jeremy P. Tarcher, Inc., Los Angeles.

Tart, Charles T., editor. *Altered States of Consciousness.* Garden City, NY: Doubleday, 1972. See especially Kilton Stewart's chapter, "Dream Theory in Malaya."

Ullman, Montague, and Zimmerman, Nan. *Working with Dreams.* Los Angeles: Jeremy P. Tarcher, Inc., 1979. Original copyright held by Delacorte Press, New York, 1979.

Articles

Ditlea, Steve. "The Dream Machine: Artificial Intelligence," *Omni,* October 1987.

Fadiman, Anne. "Stephen LaBerge: The Doctor of Dreams," *Life,* November 1986.

Keeton, Kathy. "Interview with Eric Willmot," *Omni,* June 1987.

Index

A

Adler, Alfred (Dr.), 12
Adolescents, dream
	discussions with, ix-x
Age levels, dream
	discussions and, ix-x
Alpha waves, 6-7
Animals, dreaming in, 13-15
Archetypal symbols, 30-31
Art, dreams in, 17-18
Aserinsky, Eugene, 5
Association technique for
	dream investigation, 32,
	34-35
Australian aborigines, dreams
	and, 17, 19
Autosuggestion, 20
"Awake" activity in infants, 5

B

Bad dreams, 40-42
	characters in, 30
	guidelines for describing, 41
Behavior, dreams' influence
	on, 13
Benefits of dreams, 58-59
Beowulf, 38
Beta waves, 7
Bohr, Neils, 57
Bottlenose dolphins, 14
Brain waves, 6
Bridge as dream symbol, 30

C

Cars as dream symbols, 30
Characters in a dream, viii, 30

Charlotte's Web, 38
Chinese dream stories, 56
Circle as dream symbol, 30
Colors of dreams, 7-8
Creativity, dreams and, 57-58
Crossing a bridge as dream
	symbol, 30

D

"Dark Side" of self, 31
Daydreams
	collage, 46
	vs. lucid dreaming, 46
	using with dreams, 46-47
Death in dreams, 30, 38
Delta waves, 6-7
Dement, William, 5
Directing dreams,
	techniques for, 44
Discoveries from dreams,
	57-58
Dissecting dreams, 48
Drawing dream memories, 21
Dream art and dream
	creations, 17-18
Dream associations, 32, 34-35
Dream beings
	of Naskapi tribe, 17
	of Senoi tribe, 17
Dream characters, ix, 30
Dream dictionary, 36
Dream discussions,
	importance of, ix-x
Dream groups, ix-x
Dreaming intervals, 5-6
Dreaming journey, 19
Dream interpretation
	association as technique for,
	32, 34-35

dissecting dreams, 48
	guidelines, 24-25
	kids' interpretations, 48-55
	practice pages, 25-29
Dream Journal
	construction guidelines, 78-79
	guidelines for, 19-21
	practice pages, 21-23
	privacy of, x
	sample pages for, 64-77
	techniques for, 63
Dreams, benefits of, 58-59
Dream stories, 56
Dream symbols, 30-32
"Dream villains", 42

E

Electroencephalogram (EEG), 5
Evans, Christopher (Dr.), 12

F

Facts about dreams, 13
Falling in dreams, 38, 45-46
Famous dreams, 57-58
Flying
	vs. falling, 45-46
	in good dreams, 42-43
"Forever-within-a-forever" time,
	17
Freud, Sigmund, 12, 42
Friends in dreams, 16, 17, 44
Frodo the Hobbit, 38

G

Garfield, Patricia (Dr.), 40, 44
Good dreams, 42-43

About the Author

Jonni Kincher lives in Oregon with her husband and three sons. She attended California State University in San Bernardino, where she received her education in psychology. She writes: "I first became interested in psychology when I was eight years old. I have been fascinated with it ever since. While other girls my age were reading about Nancy Drew and her adventures, I was reading about Sigmund Freud and the nightly adventures of dreams. Since I could find no nonfiction psychology books written for people my age, I read from the adult section. When I grew up I remembered my early longing for information about psychology. I found out that many young people are interested in knowing about the things psychologists study. I began to write psychology designed specifically for the 9-12 year age group. My aim has always been to avoid telling children HOW to act, so that instead I could help them understand WHY behavior occurs. By understanding the logic behind behavior, your own actions and those of others begin to make a lot of sense. When behaviors make sense, they are easier to deal with.

"I have been teaching psychology to 9-12 year olds in enrichment programs since 1983. First I taught in Redlands, California. I now teach in Coos Bay and North Bend, Oregon. I have enjoyed working *with* these gifted students as well as *for* them as an advocate of gifted education. I have written for *Gifted Children Monthly* and presented my Psychology for Kids program at a California Association for the Gifted conference."

"I hope that an early exposure to psychology will inspire bright young people to study the mind and how it works. It is my belief that our future rests in unraveling the secrets of the brain. We need our best brains to put themselves to this task."

MORE FREE SPIRIT BOOKS

Stick Up for Yourself! Every Kid's Guide to Personal Power and Positive Self-Esteem
by Gershen Kaufman, Ph.D. and Lev Raphael, Ph.D.
Realistic, encouraging how-to advice on being assertive, making friends, handling bullies, becoming responsible, growing a "feelings vocabulary," making good choices, solving problems, setting goals, and more.
Ages 8–12; $8.95; 96 pp.; illus.; s/c; 6" x 9"

Also available:
A Teacher's Guide to Stick Up for Yourself
by Gerri Johnson, Gershen Kaufman, Ph.D., and Lev Raphael, Ph.D.
$14.95; 128 pp.; s/c; 8 1/2" x 11"

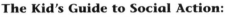

The Kid's Guide to Social Action: How to Solve the Social Problems You Choose—and Turn Creative Thinking into Positive Action
by Barbara A. Lewis
A comprehensive guide to making a difference in the world. Teaches letter-writing, interviewing, speechmaking, fundraising, lobbying, getting media coverage and more.
Ages 10 and up; $14.95; 208 pp.; illus.; B&W photos; s/c; 8 1/2" x 11"

Kidstories: Biographies of 20 Young People You'd Like to Know
by Jim Delisle
Inspiring biographies about real kids today who are doing something special to improve their lives, their schools, their communities, or the world. Includes questions to think about and resources for readers who want to know more. Ages 10 and up; $9.95; 176 pp.; B&W photos; s/c; 6" x 9"

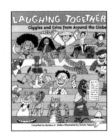

Laughing Together: Giggles and Grins from Around the Globe
by Barbara K. Walker
Hundreds of jokes, riddles, rhymes, and short tales promote multiculturalism and global awareness through laughter, the universal language. Many are printed in their original language as well as English.
For all ages; $12.95; 128 pp.; illus.; s/c; 7 1/4" x 9 1/4"

Making the Most of Today: Daily Readings for Young People on Self-Awareness, Creativity, and Self-Esteem
by Pamela Espeland and Rosemary Wallner
Quotes from figures including Eeyore, Mariah Carey, and Dr. Martin Luther King, Jr. guide young people through a year of positive thinking, problem-solving, and practical lifeskills. Ages 11 and up; $8.95; 392 pp.; s/c; 4" x 7"

Psychology for Kids: 40 Fun Tests That Help You Learn About Yourself
by Jonni Kincher
Based on sound psychological concepts, this fascinating book promotes self-discovery, self-awareness, and self-esteem. Helps you answer questions like, "Are you an introvert or an extrovert?" and "What body language do you speak?" and empowers you to make good choices about your life. Ages 10 and up; $11.95; 160 pp.; illus.; s/c; 11" x 8 1/2"

School Power: Strategies for Succeeding in School
by Jeanne Shay Schumm, Ph.D. and Marguerite Radencich, Ph.D.
Covers getting organized, taking notes, studying smarter, writing better, following directions, handling homework, managing long-term assignments, and more.
Ages 11 and up; $11.95; 132 pp.; illus.; B&W photos; s/c; 8 1/2" x 11"

It's All In Your Head: A Guide to Understanding Your Brain and Boosting Your Brain Power
by Susan L. Barrett
An "owner's manual" on the brain that kids can understand. Revised and updated edition includes new brain facts; new definitions of intelligence and creativity; new information on left- and right-brain function; new facts on how diet, exercise, and sleep affect the brain; and more.
Ages 9–14; $9.95; 160 pp.; illus.; s/c; 6" x 9"

Also available:
A Teacher's Guide to It's All in Your Head
by Susan Barrett
$6.95; 52 pp.; s/c; 8 1/2" x 11"

To place an order, or to request a free catalog of SELF-HELP FOR KIDS® materials, write or call:

Free Spirit Publishing Inc.
400 First Avenue North, Suite 616
Minneapolis, MN 55401-1730
toll-free (800)735-7323, local (612)338-2068

400 First Avenue North
Suite 616
Minneapolis, MN 55401-1730

612/338-2068
FAX 612/337-5050

ORDER TOLL-FREE
1-800-735-7323
Monday thru Friday
8:00 A.M.–5:00 P.M. CST

1 ☐ **PLEASE SEND ME THE FREE SPIRIT CATALOG**

2 NAME AND ADDRESS

NAME _____

ADDRESS _____

_____

CITY/STATE _____ ZIP ☐☐☐☐☐

3 SHIP TO (if different from billing address)

NAME _____

ADDRESS _____

_____

CITY/STATE _____ ZIP ☐☐☐☐☐

4 DAYTIME TELEPHONE _____ (in case we have any questions)

5

TITLE	PRICE	QTY.	TOTAL

6 TOTAL

SHIPPING & HANDLING

For merchandise
totals of:......................Add:
Up to $10.00 ....$3.00
$10.01–$19.99...........$4.00
$20.00–$39.99...........$4.75
$40.00–$59.99...........$6.00
$60.00–$79.99...........$7.50
$80.00–$99.99...........$9.00
$100.00–$149.99....$10.00
$150 or more...............exact
shipping charges

Orders outside continental
North America **add**
$15.00 AIR MAIL

7 SUBTOTAL _____

8 SALES TAX
(6.5% MN ONLY) **+** _____

9 SHIPPING
& HANDLING **+** _____

10 TOTAL **$** _____

TO RECEIVE A FREE COPY OF THE FREE SPIRIT
CATALOG, OR TO OBTAIN FREE SPIRIT
PUBLICATIONS, PLEASE COMPLETE THIS FORM,
ORDER BY TELEPHONE (1-800-735-7323)
OR ASK FOR FREE SPIRIT BOOKS AT YOUR
LOCAL BOOKSTORE.

THANK YOU FOR YOUR ORDER!

SEND TO: Free Spirit Publishing Inc., 400 First Ave.
North, Suite 616, Minneapolis MN 55401-1730

OR CALL: 1-800-735-7323
LOCAL: 612-338-2068, **FAX:** 612-337-5050

We offer discounts for quantity purchases.
Write or call for more information.

METHOD OF PAYMENT

☐ CHECK ☐ P.O. ATTACHED ☐ VISA ☐ MASTERCARD GOOD THROUGH ☐☐ – ☐☐

ACCOUNT # ☐☐☐☐☐☐☐☐☐☐☐☐☐☐☐☐

SIGNATURE _____